D1232348

check points

check points

Michael Casey

Adastra Press
Easthampton • Massachusetts

Library of Congress Control Number: 2011936181

The poems in this book are fictional works of imagination. Any resemblance in the poems to living or dead persons or to real events is entirely coincidental.

Acknowledgments: Thanks to the publications that first published the following: *Birmingham Poetry Review:* "name calling," "check point," "Bagley removes a thought;" *Borderlands:* "skypig;" *The Boston Phoenix:* "John on jeep hood;" *Colere:* "a poem for Mary Tyler Moore;" *College English:* "fragging," "sniperscope;" Longhouse Broadsides: "Sergeant Le's watch," "Cenerizio's service," *The Minnnesota Review:* "Bagley's sign;" *Mouth:* "drunk at the Sydney airport;" *New York Quarterly:* "95th Evac;" *The Poetry Conspiracy:* "girls at war;" *Prairie Schooner:* "shotgun ride;" *Pyramid:* "JohnJohn back at the Chu Lai Airport;" *Quarterly Review of Ideology:* "perimeter;" *Salmagundi:* "FNG," "go market," "officers' club;" *San Diego Writers Monthly:* "sniper;" *Solo:* "moving body parts;" *Witness:* "An Tan," "don't mention it," "helmet liner," "Texas Across the River."

Several of the poems appeared in the limited edition chapbook *Raiding a Whorehouse* (Adastra Press 2004).

Designed by Gary Metras in Palatino 11/17

Adastra Press
16 Reservation Road
Easthampton, MA 01027

contents

checkpoint

OK I see the dog tags
but I know you know
you need a helmet on
and flak jacket on
before you leave the LZ
so it good you know this so
I don't even
have to tell you
   Bagley starts the shit
   how he's an MP too
   what right I have
   tell him what to do
and I go
the Captain ask me
make a head count of pees
leaving the LZ
   so I point to Bagley
   and say
one

raiding a whorehouse

the jeep stops and then the three quarter ton and I notice
the left lace of my jungle boot untied but I hear shots and
so I run into the hooch *sin thay xe jip* I yell to Hieu   I run
through several rooms where there are only children and
then down a hallway nobody there then out a back door
an American behind the door are you an American? I ask
real smart he's twice my size he might be a dink drop
what's in your hands he has nothing hands against the
wall nothing Clock the honcho asks any others? I don't
know I stopped when I found him more shots out farther
back ruffpuffs show up with two Americans scared beau-
coups tell em to stop shooting tell em to stop we gotta
frisk them Clock oh yeah I got a forty-five under my belt
in front oh yeah thanks for telling me   into the three
quarter ton jeep goes first the three quarter ton stalls
Clock stop the jeep stop the jeep the jeep goes on without
us John begins his let's let em go act the youngest QC
Giang says the ruffpuffs will never work with us again we
give them go Giang doesn't let us forget he was in the field
wears a Marine field cap Giang is hard ass with Ameri-
can prisoners the prisoners and Giang and I all start
pushing the three quarter ton we get tired and have to rest
in front of the house of Miss Huynh Thi who saw us she
wears short shorts to bed she tells me I would not know
otherwise no *gai diem* her she says later she saw me
pushing the three quarter ton you push truck beaucoups
funny hell but I did not see her at the time back at the

10

provost marshall's the big guy that was shivering behind he door acts hard core   I work for the Army Post Office he says   what's your name   and then reads my shirt nametag and says I gonna remember that   I say knock yaself out   he says y'aint gonna get any mail from now on   I tell him step outside say that   he says   oh no just don't expect any mail from now on Turnwald   it's Turnwald's shirt I am wearing see   Turnwald left incountry three months before ETS freedom bird back to world   I laugh at hard core and notice my left shoelace is still untied but nothing trips up John P. Fogerty   himself or his mail   you know what I mean   you know I am saying what I am saying

anthem

second most popular song
for our unit
third platoon of the 23rd Military Police Company
was Ten Years After's
"If You Should Love Me"
but the most popular
number one *quodie* song
always blaring from our hooches
was a tribute to John Fogerty
no, it wasn't the "Fortunate Son"
it was "Proud Mary"
as soon as the song finished playing
there was an added chorus
a unit leitmotif
yaint got that song
on that fuckin tape deck again
yet?
there was a fist fight
when someone said Fogerty
in real life
evaded the draft

JohnJohn back at the Chu Lai Airport

right at the R&R center
they asked us   this is true
to fill out a piece of paper
saying why we came to Bangkok
and one guy put down "TO FUCK"
and they made him go back
and fill out another one
that wasn't obscene
wanta know what Honest John
wrote down?
Honest John didn't want to put down
any bulljiving you know
what it is
is what I wanted to write down
so I just wrote down
the reason I came to Bangkok
was
not for the bus tours

Bagley's last chips

John, when you were on your R&R
someone stole your last can of potato chips
aint that bitchy
it is getting you can't trust nobody
with anything these days
and has to be some king of royal scumbags
steal your last can of barbecue potato chips
hid in the exceedingly nasty laundry bag
under your bunk
behind where the rat's nest was
I would not want to stick my hand back there
you would have to use a broom handle

seven letters for Harmon

Harmon, listen up
you aint here yet, troop
I got seven letters today, Harmon
seven whole letters
you git no letters today
zeero letters yesday
and zeero letter the day fore that
you don't know seven people
in the whole world
might want write to you
let alone seven people
know how to write
hey
troop
quit it, Harmon
keep y'grubby hands
off my letters

shotgun ride

Lonnie Kingman is telling you
to get on you steel pot
bandolier
MP brassard
sixteen and flak jacket
MP brassard I say that twice
so as you can ride shotgun
oh no you don't sit with the driver
Lonnie Kingman do that
Lonnie Kingman say
Lonnie Kingman shotgun rider one
you shotgun rider number two
we did that before
only one shotgun
Lonnie Kingman himself
just one rifle up front
half the prisoners
leave out the back
before Lonnie
could figure out beans
when the bag was opened

Chicom

a young woman prisoner
at the POW stockade
the chopper gunner had given us
her knapsack
the girl had been hiding in mud
but inside the backpack
it was immaculate
clean clothes nicely folded
a toothbrush and at the bottom
three Chicom grenades
we call ordinance
and counterintelligence officer
spoke to the guys
asked if they would defuse a grenade
for a souvenir
ordinance guy said sure
and tried to pull
the bamboo tube
out of the serrated metal cone
it didn't work
so he started banging the grenade
viciously against a corner of the jeep
I have to say
it was riveting
I add I was a discrete distance away
but eight thousand miles
would have been better

be afraid, brother

Baby San
has no rank insignia
he is in counterintelligence
and calls hisself an agent
asks us to call him mister
one day Baby San tells Klingman
and Lonnie tells me
bring in the prisoner *Ha Si*
so I go out and say *Ha Si*
and beckon
underhanded
to follow me
Vietnamese beckon overhanded
to their animals
I have to notice
the guy is feeble
why the fuck
did the First of the Sixth
bring this one in
prisoner has one arm withered
and one eye frozen
to a spot above my hair
prisoner is also shaking
I whisper to him
khong co so, anh
I ask Mister Baby San
what's the story

with that frail guy *Ha Si*
and Baby San knows everything
looks at me like I am
monolingual
says that wasn't his name
that was his rank

shotgun rider two

Lonnie tells me
the prisoner run
don't mean nothing
there's beaucoup
most of them civilian detainees
just couple armed draft dodgers
   this time again
I am in the back
of the three quarter ton
but now there's a lot of prisoners
I am at the very back
on one of the benches
right arm holding rifle
the stock on thigh
and the left arm holding
on to the railing
the prisoner to my left
puts his right arm around my shoulder
to prevent me from falling off
no no can't do that
khong the duoc   khong the duoc
   I tell Bagley about it later   big mistake
I asked him
why didn't the prisoner
just push me off the truck and book
and Bagley thinks
he thinks and says you know
half these gooks are queer

Turnkey Bagley

really very embarrassing for our unit
entrusted with POW cage security
not a break out
a break in
the concertina wire
and fence cut through
with wire cutters
and the MP shift
on duty
belatedly catches
three H Troops
trying to get to some field whores
Bagley brags
to the platoon leader
I caught them
almost right away
from their laughing
which woke me up
just as soon as I heard it
if not earlier

dog cemetery

seeing the man
praying at the dog cemetery
Bagley yells out
you wanta believe in dog heaven, man
you go right ahead, man
knock yaself out, man
and we drive closer
and the guy looks up
and he is an officer
the officer in charge
of the scout dog platoon
his look at you
just regular
would freeze you
and this time he is really mad
and Bagley drives
that jeep away very fast
but this is an MP jeep
has 23rd MP Company
written all over it
even covering the spare tire on the back
and now which MP do you think
did the lieutenant blame for this?
every single one
he'd drive by in his jeep
past the MP bunker
at the main gate

and look at you
like you was worth
absolutely nothing
if you didn't believe in dog heaven

name calling

Daypurty Dawg
wasn't the name of the jeep exactly
but it was the caption
under the cartoon painting
on the spare tire cover
of the jeep
of the Deputy Adjutant General

the Mid Night Special wasn't
the name of a jeep either
it was the name
on the machine guns' shield
set up on the quad fifty truck

now the verbal phrase
Shine a Light on You
that was a vehicle
it was on the spotlight jeep
associated with the Mid Night Special

the etymology?
from a Leadbelly song
as in
Jody, we hold you, son
in special regard, boy
the midnight special
shine it ever loving light on you
soon

place names, north south

hill five niner

Ky Chanh

LZ Fat City

Ly Tin

Sam Tin

An Tan

Chu Lai

  Main PX

  Company HQ

  95 Evacuation Hospital

LZ Cherry Hill

LZ Bayonet

LZ Gator

Nuoc Mau

Binh Son

LZ Dottie

Quang Ngai City

  MACV Compound hamburger stand

Miss An Tan

Albert says he saw
a new girl in the ville
dep lam   very beautiful
works in the laundry
near the bookstore
in An Tan
I asked him
  is she short?
  have long black hair?
you seen her?
  hair is parted in the middle?
  and she has slant eyes?
he accuses   you did see her
  and when she walks she lifts one foot up
  and then the other?
and here Albert gets mad
some people catch on slow
some people catch on slower
I guess I should be circumspect though
Albert leaves his catch on auto

hit and run

an ARVN   a pedestrian
is hit by a jeep in Binh Son
and the Vietnamese hospital
is just around the corner
but his comrades all a bit drunk want to go
to the American hospital
Interpreter Sergeant Giang
explains this to Antonio and me
and one ARVN
pulls out a grenade
and is holding the pin
the crowd disappears
along with Interpreter Sergeant Giang
and Antonio starts yelling
at the ARVN with the grenade
who's yelling back *xe jip My   xe jip My*
I am trying to get Antonio away
and debate with the ARVN too
but the interpreter is gone
I figure out   the ARVN
is saying American jeep American jeep
and I get it
xe jip Viet I tell him   Vietnamese jeep
and the guy puts the grenade away
truthfully I didn't know
what jeep did it but I know one thing
Interpreter Sergeant Giang
is not a friend of mine

John on jeep hood

yoyoyoyo   sound of duckherds
the mud flats of Sam Tin
the barefoot children
two feet tall with twenty foot bamboo poles
herding livestock
occasionally one kid
one water buffalo
but mostly ducks
twenty   thirty   a hundred
yoyoyoyo
John sits on the jeep hood
waving at children
left and right
pointing benignly
hello hello looking good, kid
looking good   like that shirt
or authoritatively
best be advised
look sharp, dudes
where's you hat?
troop, why aint you in school?
why aren't your boots laced?
not gonna get nowhere, Joe
not tying your shoes
you lazy bum
hey, do you know where I can find some ducks?
you ask

why one kid can herd fifty animals
each with its very own mind albeit dim?
why those animals don't go every which way?
I answer
thing is
you just herd the chief duck
and all the stupid buddies follow
yoyoyoyo

demo pit

Vietnamese kids would sift
through the dirt at the firing range
and turn in unexploded grenade heads
for the bounty
MP's at the gate were
to call the counterintelligence agents
for the reward
and if they weren't around
to write out a receipt
the kids would
ask the agents
for *beaucoups tien*
and I remember Mister Byrne's
standard reply *toi ngeo lam*
I am very poor

I remember once
five grenade heads in a plastic baggie
and my hand shaking
after I bring the bag to the demo pit
shaking when I write out the receipt
after

I remember   Interpreter Sergeant Giang
telling me
write out the receipt before
bringing grenade to the demo pit

moving body parts

I stop at nineteen
in the impossible cribbage score
I'd see them there often
along the side of QL One
the victims of lesser battles
smaller victories
minor triumphs
I stopped counting
thinking I'd be able to forget easier
after I stopped counting
but now
I am losing the distinctions
and I remember every one
some more than others
nary a victor in sight
except once
a sullen militia man
emptying a magazine into a skull
dude, hey, he only had one life
to die for his country
every bullet killing a dozen flies
portions of the vanquished
shot any distance
covered with flies almost immediately
the time I carry an arm
from the middle of the road
   a unit joke
who's the man with three hands

non-judicial punishment

Parker says to me want to see something
and shows me a little brick of what looks like
pressed peat
thereon an imprint of a crown logo
right in the middle
he says that's the Thai government stamp
of purity for this brick of hash
   much later   he's worried
he confides in me   CID wants to talk
I say that brick is long gone no?
no no it isn't that it's something else
the something else
was that
Park bought a cheap radio
threw out the insides
and stuffed it with a local product
Binh Son one hundreds
he mails this package to a high school friend
it's the sniff dog's day off
and the package gets through the mails
and the contents enjoyed
but the friend's mother is not a friend of Park
and turns over all the correspondence
she finds from Park to her son
the letters definitely relate to being
around dope in country
if not exactly any kind of export import deal

Park is filled with panic
   I don't know what to say
easy I say
you say nothing
you want to see a lawyer
   bingo it works or I think it did
I never talk to him again
but know he's not court martialed
not a special court martial
not a general court martial
neither
they just non-judicial punish
his ass into the infantry
I did see him though once
he was on stand-down with his new unit
at the Chu Lai PX
I waved   from the MP jeep and
he did not wave back or nothing
he was with new friends then
and to the grunts
MP's are worth shit

sniperscope

they assign Dutch
on a bunker at LZ Bayonet
with a wonder of research
it lets you see in the dark
ruining the retina if used
for more than ten consecutive minutes
but this particular machine
had had time in grade
and there was
no way to attach the M-16
the fastenings if any
having been long lost
sergeant says
this instrument
cost two three K
you lose your ass
in the grass
before you lose
this here sniperscope
he says it twice
he sounded like a librarian
who didn't like
to loan out his book

bolo

the Captain asks me
were you aiming to shoot
the pistol out of that guy's hand?
and I said
fuck no, sir
I was aiming
for the finger I shot off

helmet liner

once was an AWOL
at the provost marshal's
and he is on his back groaning
and Desk Sergeant Ford
is upset because in the struggle
Ford says
he knocked off my helmet liner
Ford leans over the guy
restrained on the ground
Ford says to him
you knocked off my helmet liner
and punches him in the face
and then Ford grabs the canvas straps
inside the helmet liner
and punches the AWOL in the face
with the helmet liner
repeatedly
three of us are
restraining the AWOL and we yell to Goody
stop him stop him
and Goody grabs Ford
around the middle to pull him away
and Ford goes
I won't hit him anymore I promise
let me go
and Goody believes him lets him go

and Ford stomps his jungle boot
down on the AWOL's nose
Ford adds
that wouldn't happen
you didn't knock off my helmet liner

fragging

at the provost marshal's office
Taper or someone
called in a fragging
at the First of the Fourteenth
the week before the first sergeant
of B Company, Twenty-third Engineers
was knocked out of bed
by grenade concussion
my partner says to me
this kind of crime
is getting to be epidemic
it must be catchy
and it's entirely
from electromagnetic disturbances
in the atmosphere
like I'm dumb he yells out
sunspots sunspots

field grade

called over to A Company, First of the Sixth
there's two men rolling in the dirt
not punching each other but each
making every effort
to wrestle the other still
and there a pack of officers
standing by watching
and doing absolutely shit
albeit it happens
one of the wrestlers is an officer
trying to get a troop
to go to the chopper pad
the troop is refusing to go to the field
but with the two men wrestling
covered with sand and dirt and dust
they look exactly alike
and all the company grade gentlemen
watching doing nothing
to help a brother
they looked separate and apart
their uniforms still very very clean

downtown residential An Tan

downtown residential An Tan
a child five six years walks up to me
and shrieks *may gio ruoui?*
I look at him
he screams *may gio ruoui?*
he's asking me what time is it
I look at my watch
and while I can tell time thank you
I have trouble
with the thirty-five past two in the afternoon
in my Vietnamese
the child seems to have trouble too
reading the dial on my wrist
he slips the watch off and away
and books into the crowd
my Seiko never more seen
big joke of Albert thereafter
asking me what time it is
he don't know
because he don't have any watch
he says I should have known better
stopping the jeep
in that Catholic neighborhood   again

Bagley's hooch

first time on night shift
at the end of twelve hours
Lonnie brings me into Bagley's hooch
says to me this hooch used to belong
to long range reconnaissance
and Lon goes to the foot of Bagley's bunk
lifts up the bed six inches and drops it
do this ten times
or maybe twelve thirteen times
Bagley wake up then
that's the onlyest way wake up Bagley

Bagley later tells me
I saw a ghost last night
it was a long range LURP
left behind
looking for the guys left him
and get this   this guy
used to live in my hooch
ghost stood at the foot of my bed
and lifted it up a hundred times
to then drop it
and this ghost
had the fucking balls
try and wake me up

Army Commendation

Bagley cuts a hole
in the bottom of a paper cup
and sticks one of his fingers through it
and then walks over to Stanley
Miss Huynh Thi Loan
and says, Stanley, look see what
I cut off a dead gook
Stanley is horrified
and runs screaming into
the outhouse occupied
by our platoon leader captain
   I was in country six months
when the entire unit
everyone in it received
an Army Commendation Medal
everyone but Bagley
and he still can't figure out why

95th Evac

I saw it, man
a very hurt individual
hurting, man
he's on a plastic something
on top a trolley
and they are all over him, man
the tubes of blood and fluid
whatnot and gauze
sponging up blood
some of it bubbling
and he's little
you would not think
there that much blood
and then another chopper
this time
the wounded is American
the orderlies move the enemy individual
and they don't exactly throw him
but slide him quick
plastic sheet and all
on the floor
against the wall
and this American was hurting more
bigger you know
he had more blood to lose

combined action group

the Ky Chanh CAG unit
was not hurt
but the local militia was hit
grenades thrown night time
into the houses
of the commanding sergeant
and assistants
the local school house as well
the Marines in the CAG
were billeted in the school yard
we gave one of the Marines
a lift to Chu Lai
he said an assistant *trung si*
saved their ass
woke up the sleeping guard
at the school yard
and talking reaction force city
they nailed a gook squad
in the open
the proof   eight bodies
at the side of QL One
no feature recognizable
where M-sixteen magazines
are emptied into each face

John asks to stop the jeep
by the enemy dead

he sees and grabs
an awfully stained bush hat
souvenir he says
I think on the ride back
how the CAG Marine
doesn't know any Vietnamese
assistant *trung si*
would be *ha si*
same same corporal
how could the American
live in a village
not know that
John says to me
don't worry
I'll wash the hat
before I wear it

sniper

the M-79 blooker grenade launcher
the Rugers that recon units used
Valentine's Spanish Star pistol
I picked up a hitchhiker once
a sniper
and he looked like hell
but capable   an Asian-American
the only one I see in our army
a sixteen with built-on silencer
brass tacks on the stock
your kills? I ask
he goes no   I received this
from my predecessor
they might be kills
but they are not my kills
what else would they be?
I have to say it impresses the hell out of the natives
I say
I suppose you call it a nickname
Betsy or something   something like that
im he says
hip I says a double metaphor
calling a rifle silence in Vietnamese
that's what it does to people
and the rifle itself has a silencer
no he says   *IM* he says
I'm telling you to keep quiet

Victor

my Victor November friend and me
his arm would not move
would not go around and
so my arm is around his shoulder
they suggested
I close my eyes to look like his
and then they backed up the jeep
to take the picture looking down
and that is why the ground
is the actual background for the picture
except for that and the flies
the picture they took
makes both of us look alive

skypig

hey, company at Chu Lai
has a chopper now
it is the military police helicopter
Dutch promptly dubs the thing
skypig
and the name took
it flew all over the division

tracers

you didn't have to be there
it might look nice at night
the flares   parachute and star cluster
and tracer rounds
every fourth bullet from a machine gun
a red light
appearing from the distance
as part of a dotted line
from chopper towards the ground
from LZ Bayonet we saw
LZ Gator get hit real bad
if you didn't have to be there
it'd be beautiful

perimeter

from the flares and sixteen fire
something going on interesting
but it was happening
the far side of the perimeter
and then three cracking noises
and a whistle
and Buch says   that's a AK bullet
going over your head, man
he tells me to shut off the light
at the check point
and get behind the sand bags
I mean this was Buch speaking to me
dingdongdoofus
world's only Avon man
water-him-every-other-day stupid
he has to tell me to hide
how smart that made me feel
things get tough
and I must listen to a fool

floor show

we'd escort the floor show
from and back to Chu Lai
and help the girls
off the truck
if we could   sometimes
or often they did not want us to touch them
the bar girls at the club
would be there to greet them
the girls gave each other brief hugs hello
and I was left there
watching a sisterhood and its act
out of it
hugless
different page different book
sniff   dry your tears

Stanley avoided the EM clubs after
an unfortunate incident
and would waitress only the officers' club
until fired
but she'd always asked about the show
and the dancing girls
the next day
she was very curious
talking to me privately
  they girl at NCO club
  at EM club show

what they wear?
like the Checkmates Limited
an Australian band   with two dancers
of course I didn't remember
short red skirts metallic fabric
silver tassels white boots
sleeveless almost shoulderless tops
except for narrow straps
neither with time in grade
both very pretty and young
and neither could dance
this was when the youngest nurse
at the 95th Evac was really old
twenty-four or twenty-five

Winoweh
La Bamba
My Girl
A Boy Named Sue
Galveston
We Gotta Get Out of This Place

and one show had Phillippino musicians
but Vietnamese Janes for dancers
these girls were very thin
and one of them was staring at Buch
for song after song
and at the band's break time
she snuggles up to him
and they sneak back into a corner

really making out
til Buch swears and yells
furiously and dumps
the dancer on the floor
and starts kicking the dancer
I have to tell you
the dancer was not a girl at all
we   some of the pees   stop Buch
and we're laughing about the matter
later until he shows up with his M-sixteen
locks and loads
what a piece of something
an American could have got hurt

officers' club

Albert drives the jeep
by the main gate
with Stanley in back
her eyes red and damp   cheeks wets
but she is not crying just then
she's just looking at me
waiting for me to say something mean
I just log Albert's name and Stanley's name
and the jeep number on the clip board list
and Albert goes
I gotta drive Stanley home
the officers' club
don't want Stanley there no way no how
Stanley says nothing
and I was thinking of a y'all shuddup, Albert
and then thought that
Stanley's gravelly laugh
likely too much for the serious drunks
I'd told her not to go there ever
a nasty place
on a hill with a near constant   mild breeze
leather bar stools and picture windows
overlooking the South China Sea
chromed AK forty-sevens under glass
and officers there
blood on every groping paw

go market

Hieu and I return from the market
and I was pleased as anything
I bought this straw hat see
with a poem in Chinese type script
between layers of straw
visible if held up to light
with a silhouette drawing
of a boat beside the poem
all for five dollars MPC
   proudly show this purchase to Stanley
who asks how much I paid
and then gives a disgusted look
and says something awful
to Hieu in Vietnamese
and to me she says
   sowwy dude
   I get for two dollar, boy
   get you head
   out you ass sometime OK
sometimes Stanley was so nice
and sometimes she wasn't
   next time she asks me
to give her go An Tan
go market buy noodle
I knew what I was going to say
wanna go home with me, Stanley
work in my mess hall forever?

girls at war

two girls worked at the PMO as matrons
we called them Stanley and Ollie
Stanley's real name was Loan
Loan's father   a village chief   slept
in a different house every night
you know why   right?
seventeen year Loan
left us for a three day weekend
of military training
and company at Chu Lai
sent a replacement matron
to our LZ
search women workers
and prisoners
Loan had two opinions of the training
there was too much exercise
she was very tired   *met lam quodie*
and then another time
she explained lots of girls there
she never see beaucoup long time
and they talktalk all night
it beaucoup fun time
she liked the shooting part
and did so well
they gave her the flag to carry
at the closing ceremony
   anyway I was talking to Dutch

I wasn't talking to her at the time
but why can't I shut the fuck up
I says to Dutch glib like
was it worth your father gets killed
and for that
you get to carry a lousy flag
and Loan's hearing was fantastic
I didn't even know
she was nearby the next room
she overheard every word
and why can't I keep the fuck quiet
she yells at me in tears
if she knew how to shoot before
no one'd be able get close enough
throw the grenade killed her father
and that's not what I meant at all

FNG

with one after another
of my friends or comrades
she'd develop a crush
but never with me
it never bothered me of course
schoolgirl enamorments
with very short shelflives
with John she found a condom in his wallet
with Albert pictures of two girlfriends in *Hoa Ky*
with Bagley a picture of a Vietnamese girl
and then the new guy shows up
from the 82nd Airborne
why she have to love him
and not me
his prior unit left in country
and left Slick to transfer to ours
really goodlooking scum
looked like Robert Frost in a football helmet
the crush with him the worst yet
yet more giggles and whispers
sickening
what did he say about her
   he think I ugly
   I stupid I talk too much
   give me tell me plee
   what he say me

war movie

I'll never know how it turned out
but you can always tell
how lousy a movie is
by how many English actors are in it
and this movie had problems
firstly the NCO club next door
was all out of cans of potato chips
regular or barbecue
they had neither
then seemed like every actor was English
and another thing it was too long
a four reel film
and the projectionist took his time
changing reels in our wall-less theater
like a car port
the only real enclosure
the projectionist booth
the audience diminished too
and then left   *didi'*d
I am the only one left
me the audience
and the crap for brains projectionist
says that Chu Lai
forgot to send the last reel
the lying little shit jokes
this war ended early

Texas Across the River

the news spread quick
a western at the movies
not first run
but a real authentic cowboy film
the dink interpreters knew about it
the gook kid filling sandbags
the kid I gave soap and toothpaste to
even he knows about it
he says to me
number ten picture
you give me don't go
but I was gonna go
I arrange for Bagley to wake me up
Bagley forgets all about me
and the theater is blown up
two separate charges
within fifteen minutes
I talk to Bagley at the hospital about it
he says
how'd that gook know
it was such a lousy movie?

don't mention it

first of all you don't refer
to scars on someone's face
and you don't mention to Dano
anything about cute Vietnamese kids
just don't do it
don't say a single syllable OK?
for one thing he might be
on the down side of being
awake for three days
for another   in the field
once this little kid walks up to us
throws a grenade   beats feet
Dano didn't even see the kid
we had to tell him about it later
why his face looks
like someone scraped it
with a grate-o-matic
didn't even see the grenadier
Dano was unconscious
before hitting the ground
the kid on the other hand was dead
before he hit the ground
so just eat your can of potato chips
and shut the fuck up OK?

a poem for Mary Tyler Moore

day before the theater blew up
the movie there was so bad
it was never released in the states
it was *What's So Bad About Feeling Good*
it has a bird from South America
spreading a virus throughout the USA
and the virus makes people nice
to each other and good natured in general
and before everyone knows it
tobacco sales plummet
and the tobacco industry goes up in smoke
against this insidious affliction
and the firearm companies go bankrupt
and the alcohol industries
can't sell its gutrot
so Wall Street buys off the government
to fight this disease
and the contagion
spreads to other countries
and the Pentagon is furious
with the virulence of this condition
and all these vital institutions
gang up together to kill the bird
whereupon the heroine Norma Normal
who bought the original bird
finds an egg on a pillow

and there is hope again
in the world of this crummy movie
    the next day the theater went up
two separate explosive charges
one to kill the audience
the other to kill the people
taking care of the audience

gynecologist

to avoid unpleasantness
officers would stay away from the EM club
but this never occurred to Major Medino
whenever there was a floor show
because there was nothing
as wonderful as live entertainment
specially when
there were gogo girls dancing
   now none of the enlisteds minded this
and everyone liked Major Medino
he was the only doctor
on our landing zone
and some troop would always
request *La Bamba*
of the floor show band
in the Major's honor
Sutton tells me that because
the Major was Spanish was why
he got sent to our shitty LZ
where he did such yeoman service
on two particular days
when the sappers hit us
April Fool's and also earlier when
the theater was blown up
Sutt tells me that by training and trade
he was a gynecologist
back in the world

and so one night on the LZ
when the pregnant whore
was pushed off the deuce and a half
and was really really hurting
it was because Major Medino
was there that she
was one lucky woman
that's what Sutt says
if you want to believe it
I mean if you were a pregnant whore
pushed off a truck
I believe you'd be luckier
not to be there to begin with

Cenerizio's service

the only time all of us
the platoon together
I recall wondering
if John's night shift
from the cage would show
they do   every single richard
and National Policeman Hieu
ARVN QC Hau
National Police Highway Patrolman Long
Interpreter Sergeants Tuats, Son, and Giang
from intelligence
and company at Chu Lai
sends a dozen bodies
to man the gate, the Provost Marshal's Office
the north south patrols, the monkey house
Crazy Rusty relieves me
at the gate
I thank him
de nada he says
at the chapel all there to hear
Father Bykowski's mass
all his parishioners
there for the combat zone confession
bread and wine
for the unit and attached
except for the dead Cenerizio

and Interpreter Sergeant Le
killed in the same bunker
the same night
the same hour same minute
maybe not the same second
but you know it was close very close

Sergeant Le's watch

No Neck walks over
with the gook lieutenant
in charge of the interpreters
Sergeant Le   you know him
die
him father give him watch
give him ask plee who take watch
father want him back you know
   I said I knew the medics
at the aid station
the First of the Fourteenth Artillery
and I said
while I couldn't promise
I would try to find the watch
I lied

good bye jest

maybe just a gesture
a so long guest
kind of thing
an unsubtle threat more likely
at one of the remote LZ's
maybe Sally or Siberia
the colonel
our own *dai ta*
in his chopper
is leaving the LZ
and you hear it
the shots
a whole M-sixteen being emptied
complete magazine
the fire from within our wire
nothing happened
from this *beau geste*
what kind of officer
would report his own guys
shot at him and missed

Bagley removes a thought

Bagley dumps on Antonio one particular time
Bagley sees Antonio
sitting   leaning forward
and moving his skull
in something of a circle
shaking his head
and Bagley asks him
why   he says
I am removing a thought
and so Bagley scoffs and disparages
so this the fucking irony
later after Cenerizio is killed
I see Bagley
at the Provost Marshal's
and he's sitting on the backsteps
leaning forward
turning his head sideways
hitting the ear opposite the ground
with his hand
slapping himself hard
and you know
I knew right away exactly
what he wasn't thinking of

personal effects

typed:

  page four of four

  bottle, plastic, orange malaria pills, one

  bottle plastic, white malaria pills, one

  jungle wallet, Americal Division emblem, one

  finger nail clippers, one

  string of beads, plastic, multi-colored, two

  photoposter, 2' x 3', girl in white bathing suit

   inscribed, "ALL MY LOVE, CATHY/ HOW DO I LOOK, GREG?" one

written:

  on diagonal line across page

    NOTHING MORE FOLLOWS

pentagon

in country the My Lai tragedy
occurred before my time
and the lesser known Seymour Hersh story
on Ky Chanh, Quang Tin Province,
was before my time as well
but my patrol route
on Highway One
was through Ky Chanh
and I remember once near Ky Chanh
seeing children play with a stick and ball
with what looked like a pitcher's mound and a home plate
and then there were four bases
now I wish I had stopped
taught them something about the game
but that would mean time travel
you can't get there from now

Cape San Jacques

there
over a thousand soldiers
swam for the American warship
he and ten others
reached the vessel
he remembers Captain Bagley well
and Sergeant Dutch
and Casey also
but Casey's rank
he does not recall
his oldest son is a cab driver
which is a very good job
for the tourists
he is no longer a policeman
  now he is a farmer
and because
there is no trade embargo currently
he wonders if his brother Casey
would be able to invest in his farm

About the Author

Michael Casey was the Yale Younger Poet in 1972 with his book, *Obscenities*. His later collections of poetry include *Millrat*, *The Million Dollar Hole*, and *Permanent Party*. He was born in Lowell, Massachusetts and was educated at the Lowell Technological Institute and the State University of New York at Buffalo.

THE ADASTRA PRESS LIST

1979 - 2011

Zoë Anglesey, *SOMETHING MORE THAN FORCE: Poems for Guatemala, 1971-1982,* letterpress, sewn, 1982, offset 1984

Margaret Key Biggs, *PETALS FROM THE WOMANFLOWER,* ltrpr, sewn 1983

Norman R. Bissell, *STRUGGLE FOR THE DAWN,* letterpress, sewn, 1982

Martha Carlson-Bradley, *BEAST AT THE HEARTH,* letterpress, sewn, 2005

Martha Carlson-Bradley, *IF I TAKE YOU HERE,* letterpress, sewn, 2011

Martha Carlson-Bradley, *NEST FULL OF CRIES,* letterpress, sewn, 2000

Michael Casey, *CHECK POINTS,* offset, perfect bound, 2011

Michael Casey, *MILLRAT,* letterpress, sewn, 1996, expanded ed., offset, 1999

Michael Casey, *RAIDING A WHOREHOUSE,* letterpress, sewn, 2004

Alan Catlin, *SHELLEY AND THE ROMANTICS,* letterpress, sewn, 1993

David Chorlton, *THE VILLAGE PAINTERS,* letterpress, sewn, 1990

Leonard J. Cirino, *THE TRUTH IS NOT REAL,* letterpress, sewn, 2006

Merritt Clifton, *FROM AN AGE OF CARS,* letterpress, sewn, 1980

Clifton, Sagan, Ehrhart, Metras, *NUCLEAR QUARTET,* folded broadsheet, letterpress, 16"x8.5" 1980

Jane Candia Coleman, *DEEP IN HIS HEART J.R. IS LAUGHING AT US,* letterpress, sewn, 1991

Jim Daniels, *ALL OF THE ABOVE,* letterpress, sewn, 2011

Jim Daniels, *NIAGARA FALLS,* letterpress, sewn, 1994, offset, perf. 1995

Jim Daniels, *DIGGER'S BLUES,* letterpress, sewn, 2002

Jim Daniels, *DIGGER'S TERRITORY,* letterpress, sewn, 1989

Cortney Davis, *THE BODY FLUTE,* letterpress, sewn, 1994

Gregory Dunne, *HOME TEST,* letterpress, sewn 2009

W.D. Ehrhart, *BEAUTIFUL WRECKAGE: New & Selected Poems,* offset, 1999

W.D. Ehrhart, *GIFTS,* broadsheet, letterpress, 9"x 12", 2003

W.D. Ehrhart, *MATTERS OF THE HEART,* letterpress, sewn, 1981

W.D. Ehrhart, *MOSTLY NOTHING HAPPENS,* letterpress, sewn, 1996

W.D. Ehrhart, *THE OUTER BANKS & Other Poems,* letterpress, sewn, 1984, offset, perfect bound, 1984

W.D. Ehrhart, *THE DISTANCE WE TRAVEL,* letterpress, sewn, 1993, offset, perf. bound, 1994

W.D. Ehrhart, *SLEEPING WITH THE DEAD,* letterpress, sewn, 2006

W.D. Ehrhart, *WINTER BELLS,* letterpress, sewn, 1988

W.D. Ehrhart, *THE BODIES BENEATH THE TABLE,* offset, perf. 2010

Jim Finnegan, *MY ANGELS,* broadsheet, letterpress, art by Susan Finnegan, 8.75" x 11.75", 1995

Kyle Flak, *THE SECRET ADMIRER*, letterpress, sewn, 2010

David Giannini, *ANTONIO & CLARA,* letterpress, sewn, 1990

David Giannini, *AZ TWO: Words of Travel,* letterpress, sewn, 2009

David Giannini, *From ELLIPSES, PART II,* broadsheet, ltrpr, 8.75"x 11.75", 1996

Jack Gilbert, *GOING WRONG,* broadsheet, letterpress, 8.75 x 11.5", 1992

D M Gordon, *FOURTH WORLD,* letterpress, sewn, 2010

Andy Gunderson, *CITY PAUSES*, letterpress, sewn, 1980

Gertrude Halstead, *memories   like burrs,* letterpress, sewn, 2006, offset, sewn, 2006

Linda Lee Harper, *BLUE FLUTE,* letterpress, sewn, 1999

Dawnell Harrison, *VOYAGES*, letterpress, sewn, 2010

Michael Hettich, *BEHIND OUR MEMORIES,* letterpress, sewn, 2003

Harry Humes, *ROBBING THE PILLARS,* letterpress, sewn, 1984

Geoffrey Jacques, *SUSPENDED KNOWLEDGE*, letterpress, sewn, 1998

Greg Joly, *HAND LABOR,* letterpress, sewn, 1992

Greg Joly, *VILLAGE LIMITS*, letterpress, sewn, 2008

Richard Jones, *INNOCENT THINGS,* letterpress, sewn, 1985

Richard Jones, *SONNETS,* letterpress, sewn, 1990

Richard Jones, *THE STONE IT LIVES ON,* letterpress, sewn, 2000

Richard Jones, *WINDOWS AND WALLS,* letterpress, sewn, 1982

Anna Kirwan, *THE FIRST THING,* letterpress, sewn, 2001

Joseph Langland, *TWELVE POEMS with Preludes and Postludes*, letterpress, sewn, 1988, offset, perf. bound, 1989

M.L. Liebler, *BREAKING THE VOODOO,* letterpress, sewn, 2001

Christopher Locke, *HOW TO BURN*, letterpress, sewn, 1995

Thomas Lux, *A BOAT IN THE FOREST,* letterpress, sewn, 1992

Thomas Lux, *GOD PARTICLES*, offset, perfect bound, reprint, 2011

Thomas Lux, *PECKED TO DEATH BY SWANS,* letterpress, sewn, 1993

Thomas Lux, *THE BLIND SWIMMER: Selected Early Poems, 1970-1975,* offset, perfect bound, 1996

Thomas Lux, *THE DROWNED RIVER,* offset., perf. bound, reprint, 1993

D. Roger Martin, *NO DREAMS FOR SALE,* letterpress, sewn, 1983

Dawn McDuffie, *CARMINA DETROIT*, letterpress, sewn, 2006

Louis McKee, trans., *MARGINALIA: Poems from the Old Irish*, bilingual, letterpress, sewn, 2008

Gary Metras, *DESTINY'S CALENDAR*, offset, perf. bound, reprint, 1988

Gary Metras, *SEAGULL BEACH,* letterpress, sewn, 1995

Gary Metras, ed., *THE ADASTRA READER,* offset, perfect bound, 1987

Gary Metras, *THE NECESSITIES,* letterpress, sewn, 1979

Gary Metras, *THE NIGHT WATCHES*, letterpress, sewn, 1981

Michael Miller, *EACH DAY,* letterpress, sewn, 2005

Judith Neeld, *SEA FIRE,* letterpress, sewn, 1987

Ed Ochester, *ALLEGHENY,* letterpress, sewn, 1995

Ed Ochester, *COOKING IN KEY WEST,* letterpress, sewn, 2000

Ed Ochester, *THE REPUBLIC OF LIES*, letterpress, sewn, 2007

Peter Oresick, *OTHER LIVES,* letterpress, sewn, 1985, offset, perf. 1985

Stephen Philbrick, *THREE,* letterpress, sewn, 2003

Stephen Philbrick, *UP TO THE ELBOW,* letterpress, sewn, 1997

Constance Pierce, *PHILIPPE AT HIS BATH,* letterpress, sewn, 1983

David Raffeld, *INTO THE WORLD OF MEN,* letterpress, sewn, 1997

David Raffeld, *THE BALLAD OF HARMONICA GEORGE and Other Poems,* letterpress, sewn, 1989

Michael Rattee, *FALLING OFF THE BICYCLE FOREVER*, offset, 2010

Michael Rattee, *MENTIONING DREAMS,* letterpress, sewn, 1985

Michael & Kiev Rattee, *ENOUGH SAID: A Poetic Dialogue Between Father & Son,* letterpress, sewn, 2002

Susan Edwards Richmond, *BOTO,* letterpress, sewn, 2002

Susan Edwards Richmond, *PURGATORY CHASM,* letterpress, sewn, 2007

Karen Rigby, *FESTIVAL BONE,* letterpress, sewn, 2004

Becky Rodia, *ANOTHER FIRE,* letterpress, sewn, 1997

Miriam Sagan, *ACEQUIA MADRE: Through the Mother Ditch*, ltrpr, sewn, 1988

Miriam Sagan, *POCAHONTAS DISCOVERS AMERICA*, ltrpr, sewn, 1993

Charles Scott, *OLD ORDNANCE,* letterpress, sewn, 2005

Tom Sexton, *A CLOCK WITH NO HANDS,* offset, perf. bound, 2007

Tom Sexton, *LEAVING FOR A YEAR,* letterpress, sewn, 1998

Tom Sexton, *THE LOWELL POEMS,* letterpress, sewn, 2005

Laurel Speer, *DON'T DRESS YOUR CAT IN AN APRON,* ltrpr, sewn, 1981

Barry Sternlieb, *FISSION,* letterpress, sewn, 1986

Wally Swist, *ACCOMPANIMENT,* broadsheet, letterpress, 8.5" x 11", 2003

Wally Swist, *FOR THE DANCE,* letterpress, sewn, 1991

Wally Swist, *WAKING UP THE DUCKS,* letterpress, sewn, 1987

Susan Terris, *POETIC LICENSE,* letterpress, sewn, 2004

Emmet Van Driesche, *THE LAND BEFORE US: Poems of the Sea,* ltrpr, sewn, 2004

Mary Jane White, trans., Marina Tsvetaeva's *NEW YEAR'S: An Elegy for Rilke*, letterpress sewn 2007

Clarence Wolfshohl, *SEASON OF MANGOS*, letterpress, sewn, 2009